Poetry From Being

A Light Unto The Self

Copyright © 2012 by Colin Drake

First Edition

All rights reserved. No part of this book shall be reproduced or transmitted, for commercial purposes, without written permission from the author.

Also by the same author:

Beyond the Separate Self

The End of Anxiety and Mental Suffering

A Light Unto Your Self

Self Discovery Through Investigation of Experience

Humanity Our Place in the Universe The Central Beliefs of the Worlds Religions

----

Poetry From Beyond the Separate Self

These titles are available as: e-books and as paperbacks from
http://www.lulu.com/spotlight/colin108atbigponddotcom

Contents

Introduction	3
1 A Light unto Yourself	5
2 Separation is Suffering	8
3 Awakening	11
4 Each Moment Reveals the Absolute	14
5 The Myth of Doing Nothing	17
6 Restless Mind … No Problem	20
7 Memories are Made of This	23
8 Nonduality	26
9 Awakening is not an Experience	29
10 Awareness a No-Brainer	32
11 The Fundamental Secret	35
12 Awareness and Thought	38
13 Hakuin's Song of Freedom	41
14 Investigation is Experiential not Intellectual	44
15 Instruments of the Absolute	47
16 Purpose and Meaning	50
17 On This and That	53
18 Nothing Has Essential Meaning	56
19 Free Will … Myth or Reality?	59
20 The Practical Application of Awakening	62
21 You Ask For Proof	65
22 Peace and Goodwill	68

Introduction

I have been asked why write poetry after three books of prose? When discussing this with a poet friend of mine he asserted that poetry has the potential to be more powerful than prose, as it is more condensed and thus requires the reader to investigate its meaning more than prose, which tends to put the meaning 'on a plate'. As my writings are always an exhortation for the readers to investigate the Truth for themselves I was greatly attracted to this and I think that it has some validity.

These poems are inspired by chapters from my third book *A Light Unto Your Self*. The first four chapters have been re-ordered so as to give the poems a more consistent flow.

Each poem should be read slowly and carefully not moving onto the next quatrain (four line verse) until you have fully 'got' what is being offered. This may require some investigation and contemplation which is all the better for then the meaning will be your own discovery that the quatrain has pointed you to. Do not move onto the next poem until you have spent some time contemplating and considering the present one.

If you have any questions you can contact me on colin108@dodo.com.au , or alternatively buy the prose version of *A Light Unto Your Self* as an e-book, or in paperback at www.lulu.com

Poem One

A Light Unto Your Self

This poem highlights the importance of investigating one's direct experience from the view-point of 'knowing nothing', and making one's own discoveries so that one can become 'a light unto oneself'.

A Light Unto Your Self

In an early *sutta* Buddha is said to comment:

'There are seven factors of enlightenment,

Awareness of awareness, investigation of the way ...'

These first two are paramount, come what may.

The next five are outcomes of these,

Which follow naturally as a breeze,

If by investigating one becomes aware

That awareness is forever here, not rare.

For this to be really so

All 'knowing' one must let go.

The starting point is a naked mind

So we don't 'clothe' that which we find.

Dogma and beliefs must be abhorred,

Although 'pointers' need not be ignored.

There are mystical paths to follow

To be abandoned if found to be 'hollow'.

Finally one must discover the truth for oneself,

For this, 'teachings' should be left on the shelf,

Seeing clearly throughout the investigation,

Then what's found suffers no degradation.

So the discoveries that we may make,

When aware of awareness, thus awake,

Our direct experience they will be

Requiring no outside authority.

Then quotes, like those in verse one,

May be useful as confirmation.

But, as at the last Buddha said himself:

You must become 'A Light Unto Yourself'!

Poem Two

Separation is Suffering

This poem considers how identifying oneself as a separate object in a universe of separate objects leads to suffering.

Separation is Suffering

If we identify as a separate being

In a hostile universe,

Then we have no choice but seeing

Manifestation as diverse.

When we think of ourselves as an object

And others that as well,

An imaginary self-image we project,

Resulting in a personal hell.

From this mind-created suffering ensues.

Not mental or physical pain,

But the outcome of the mind which 'stews'

On these, as they wax and wane.

Of status, position, achievements, occupation,

Our individual self-image is made,

Mental prowess, appearance, family situation,

Future goals and memories that fade.

Identification with this will presage
Insecurity, angst and fear.
Postponed by bolstering this image,
Searching for 'more' to appear.

Making us live in the past or future,
Not seeing things as they 'are'.
The eternal now we cannot nurture,
And this does each moment mar.

Self-image is an imaginary, illusory construct,
Absent, there's no fear of losing face.
For with 'no self' there is nothing to protect;
This realization needs to take place.

Poem Three

Awakening

This poem considers awakening from the dream of separation.

Awakening

To awaken, rouse yourself from the dream,

Of being a separate object on the earth.

No matter how bewitching this may seem,

An illusion the ego has fostered since your birth

To see this, into your own nature enquire,

To discover the underlying strata,

Where thoughts and feelings rise, then expire.

The perceiver of this ephemeral data.

The body is experienced as a flow of sensations,

The mind as a flow of images and thought.

What is it, then, that notices these presentations?

The constant subject that need never be sought.

That which we feel we have always been,

The unchanging basis of this very life,

That which all of our moments has seen,

Our ups and downs, joys, struggles and strife.

The clue is that, to live, aware we must be

Of mind and body that seem to ebb and flow;

So Awareness, itself, is That which these see.

The changeless that doesn't come and go.

Check it out in this moment, now

Notice how thoughts and sensations to and fro,

In ever present Awareness, that is how

Our experiences we can enjoy and know.

So This is what we are, have always been.

Wake up to this fact, by truly knowing

That, which our whole life-story has seen.

A constant witnessing presence, no thing!

Poem Four

Each Moment Reveals the Absolute

This poem points to what is discovered by investigation and self-inquiry.

Each Moment Reveals the Absolute

From birth to death our life is a series

Of moment to moment experiences.

Comprising thoughts, sensations and mental images

And That which sees these in all of their stages.

A torrent of objects that come and go

In Awareness, the subject, by which we 'know'.

The constant conscious perceiving presence,

Neath body and mind, our ultimate essence.

The universal consciousness is Awareness whilst at rest,

Within which, in motion*, the cosmos is manifest.

So in Awareness all things come and go,

As in stillness all movements ebb and flow.

Awareness is ever silent and still

Witnessing all vibrations that mill…

Thus It is omniscient and omnipresent,

The substratum from which all things are 'lent'.

In which they are perceived and reside,

Omnipotent for into This they subside.

Pure and pristine, by things unaffected,

By whose radiance they are detected.

Thus the properties of Awareness that we have found

Agree with those, of the Absolute, religions propound.

Without the 'personal' which the Western ones posit

However, all persons are manifestations of It!

So It does indeed contain personal qualities,

But these are impermanent, therefore not properties.

Thus when each moment we investigate

The Absolute is revealed, totally innate.

* Cosmic energy for energy implies (is synonymous with) motion. Modern physics has shown that all matter is comprised of energy and is thus just a complex series of movements, or vibrations.

Poem Five

The Myth of Doing Nothing

This poem addresses the idea that there is nothing we can do and that everything' just happens by itself'

The Myth of Doing Nothing

A friend suffers from existential angst,

Dispelled by readings on nonduality,

Or by attending inspiring satsangs,

But anxiety returns as his normality..

It turns out there is nothing he daily does

To awaken by becoming aware.

He has been taught 'there's nothing to do', thus

His headspace remains, in despair.

Now it is true that there is 'nothing to achieve'

As Awareness is always here.

For this to be of use, and our angst relieve,

Of this we must be the seer.

It is also the case that there's 'nothing to find',
As Awareness can never be lost.
To 'end the search' we must bear this in mind,
Overlooked, it's to our great cost.

There's also nothing for us to get or acquire,
As what we would obtain we already are!
Enlightenment, awakening, that which we desire:
Is to recognize Awareness as here, never afar.

So, for there to be 'nothing to achieve, find or get',
We need to cultivate this 'seeing'.
Thus 'Awareness of Awareness' can be fully met,
And permeate our very being.

If this is not so investigate,
Until you truly 'know'.
For if you just leave this to fate,
Angst will not ease, but grow!.

Poem Six

Restless Mind? No Problem!

This poem attempts to show that although the restless mind hinders meditation, it is no problem when relaxing into pure awareness.

Restless Mind? No Problem!

When you sit to contemplate or meditate,

Do you suffer from a restless mind?

Suppressing thoughts will only exacerbate

This problem which many often find.

Especially when much concentration is needed

On a mantra, symbol or the breath.

Requiring that the thought-flow be impeded,

In this most minds are 'out of their depth'.

However, for 'relaxing into awareness' this is not so,

As there is nothing to achieve, find or get,

Just 'aware of awareness' become and know,

Then the mind may quieten in the peace that's met.

For awareness, itself, is always silent and still,

Which is the definition of peace.

When aware of this then thoughts that mill

May lessen or even finally cease.

Even if the mind continues to chatter,

Witness the thoughts, but do not follow.

They ebb and flow, don't let them matter,

Then they will be found to be truly 'hollow'.

Note the space between them and thus see

The nothingness in which they come and go.

This combined with awareness can set you free,

For 'Aware Nothingness' is The Absolute you know.

So This which great concentration may reveal,

Is by relaxing into awareness easily seen,

Needing no effort, just keeping an even keel,

Aware of the nothingness in which thoughts have been.

Poem Seven

Memory – A Two-Edged Sword

This poem shows the practical use of memory and how, when misinterpreted, it can give the illusion of a 'separate self'.

Memory – A Two-Edged Sword

An inquirer read in a book,

That memory is just a concept,

This her whole foundation shook,

"No past (self)' she could not accept.

For memory is a paradoxical thread,

On which seeming continuity revolves.

If not believed our 'story' we could shed,

And watch as our 'small self' dissolves.

However, it is a useful tool,

For living our day to day lives,

On this our knowing we spool,

Thus objects can we recognise.

Every thing that we meet,

Our mind compares with this store,

So our experience we can greet,

Informed by what's gone before.

But memories can easily create,

The illusion of a separate being,

If their meaning we overstate,

Not their impermanence seeing.

In fact they just come and go,

In the constant subjective presence,

Ephemeral objects that flow,

In Awareness, our true essence.

So, although memory has its use,

Past memories can delude,

Causing us identity to confuse,

With the story that's viewed.

Poem Eight

Nonduality

This poem shows how investigation can lead to nonduality.

Nonduality

Nonduality: 'not two' of anything,

For the term 'oneness' implies multiplicity.

No thing is permanently existing,

All fleeting movements in essential Reality.

In each of our direct experiences this can be shown,

Sense-impressions, mental-images and thought,

Appearing in Awareness by which they are known,

Into which they subside, back into naught.

Before each is Awareness of 'what is',

The totality of these in any given mo,

They are seen, by That, within this,

And That is still here after they go.

For each of us every object that we meet,

Is experienced as thought and sensation,

Seen by Awareness, thus them can we greet,

And bid them farewell at their cessation.

Awareness can be defined as consciousness at rest,

Aware of all movements that in it occur,

All things are cosmic energy, filled with this zest,

Exhausted, back into motionless they recur.

For in stillness all movements arise,

In this they abide, by Awareness are spied,

Back into this they all must subside,

When out of momentum, the end of the ride.

So there is no duality, or dissociation,

Between the unmanifest and manifestation,

For both are Consciousness, at rest or in motion,

Of the same essence, Awareness and Creation.

Poem Nine

Awakening is not an Experience

This poem highlights the fact that awakening is a recognition, or realization, rather than an experience.

Awakening is not an Experience

Experiences come and go,

In That by which our minds can know,

Thoughts and images when they show,

And sensations as they to and fro.

The Knower which is ever behind

The ephemeral body/mind.

A constant conscious subjective presence,

Our fundamental innermost essence.

For each of us the world is made,

Of experiences which appear and fade,

In Awareness which is ever here,

Closer than close, nearer than near.

If to yourself you wish to be kind,

Avoid identifying with the mind.

Just a flow of images and thought,

In That which need never be sought.

To awaken identify with the latter,

The source, ground and end of all matter.

See that you are the permanent

Awareness, and thus ever content.

This awakening is not an experience,

Nor with thoughts and images a dalliance.

A realization of That which never changes,

In which cosmic energy just re-arranges.

Many experiences may it evoke,

They varied greatly in those who awoke.

But freedom is seeing 'I am That',

And the cultivation of this fact!

Poem Ten

Awareness a No-Brainer!

This article was written in reply to the assertion that awareness cannot exist without a brain.

Awareness a No-Brainer!

A materialist critic quipped:

Awareness needs someone, who is aware,

Requiring that one be equipped,

With a brain, or else it cannot be there!

This is the central argument of the mind,

Our investigations to bedevil,

Making it more difficult to find,

Neath body/mind, the deeper level.

Awareness in which these must always be,

Thoughts, images, sensations - objects that flow,

In this subjective presence by which we see,

Our experiences as they come and go.

Showing no brain is needed is child's play.

Consider electrons whose behaviour is changed

By being observed, so we could say,

They are aware of circumstances when rearranged.

Or white corpuscles in the blood,

Attacking foreign bodies that invade,

Thus nipping illness in the bud,

By awareness of threats that could degrade.

And brainless moulds that thrive and grow,

In damp and fetid situations,

When aware of food towards it they flow,

Requiring no mental cogitations!

As Descartes said – ourselves we know,

By internal awareness of thoughts and existence,

Innate in all beings, preceding the 'show',

Of reflection, knowledge and cognizance.

Poem Eleven

The Fundamental Secret

This poem discusses a secret which is much more fundamental than that described in the movie (and book) 'The Secret'.

The Fundamental Secret

'The Secret' relies on the laws of attraction,

Using the mantra 'Ask, Believe and Receive',

To achieve abundance and satisfaction,

By mind-power and positive thoughts we weave.

However, there is a secret more fundamental,

By applying which we need no more 'stuff'.

Its power is absolute, not incremental,

Realizing that 'each moment is enough'.

The discovery that beneath the body/mind,

There is an aware subjective presence,

In which thoughts and sensations we 'find',

Our immutable, unchanging essence.

Witnessing 'what is' at any given moment,

Unaffected, not seeking to change any thing,

Thus dissatisfaction It cannot foment,

And the desire for more cannot It sting.

So we are always totally at peace,

When with Awareness identified,

The feeling of lack will completely cease,

As seeking and acquiring are nullified.

In this 'each moment is enough'

Which is a very potent, powerful tool,

To defuse the mind when feeling rough,

And negative thoughts that appear to fool.

Our boredom and insomnia it can relieve,

Mental suffering and desires which tax.

Replacing 'Ask, Believe and Receive',

With 'Investigate, Realize and Relax!'

Poem Twelve

Awareness and Thought

This poem highlights the differences between thought and awareness and shows the importance of recognizing this.

Awareness and Thought

A reader questioned the difference,

Between Awareness and thought,

So for his particular reference,

The many distinctions I sought.

A sound in the mind,

That which this hears.

Any mental image we find,

That in which this appears.

That which is witnessed,

The witness of this object.

The feeling of being stressed,

Of this the conscious subject.

All things that in the mind are seen,

That which does the seeing.

Any thing that we know has been,

The knower of this 'being'.

In the mind any movement,

The aware serenity and peace.

Self-image seeking improvement,

That in which all 'becomings' cease.

So Awareness is the constant subjective presence,

Aware of ephemeral objects that come and go,

Our innermost fundamental conscious essence,

In which thoughts and sensations ebb and flow.

Becoming aware of and identifying with This,

By direct investigation of the 'way'

Leads to awakening, leaving nothing amiss,

As in an ancient sutta Buddha did say.

Poem Thirteen

Hakuin's Song of Freedom

A beautiful expression of freedom, from the Mahayana School of Buddhism.

Hakuin's Song of Freedom

For such as, reflecting within themselves,

Testify to the truth of Self-nature,

To the truth that Self-nature is no-nature,

They have really gone beyond the ken of sophistry.

For them opens the gate of oneness of cause and effect,

And straight runs the path of non-duality and non-trinity,

Abiding with the not-particular which is in particulars,

Whether going or returning, they remain for ever unmoved.

How boundless the sky of Samadhi unfettered!

How transparent the perfect moonlight of the Fourfold Wisdom!

At that moment what do they lack?

As the Truth eternally calm reveals itself to them.

This very earth is the Lotus Land of Purity,

And this body is the body of the Buddha.

Poem Fourteen

Investigation Must Be Experiential

This poem discusses the fact that investigation/inquiry has to be experiential rather than intellectual and that the realization it produces needs to be cultivated to become established.

Investigation Must Be Experiential

Said a strident critic of self-inquiry

The deeper level of Awareness he had found,

But this had not relieved his anxiety.

As his inquiry was intellectual, not profound.

For investigation to lead to the Absolute Reality,

It must be directly experiential,

So 'awareness of awareness' becomes our normality,

And the identity change fundamental.

If of Awareness we become truly aware,

We can deeply investigate this,

Its properties we may find and compare,

Relieving angst and leading to bliss.

Effortless, for its presence requires no effort.

Choicelessly of thoughts and sensations aware.

Omnipresent, never needing to be sought.

Omniscient, seeing 'things' anywhere.

Still, aware of the slightest motion.

Silent, aware of the smallest sound,

Peaceful, of consciousness the ocean,

Radiant, by its light all things are found.

As Awareness is what we truly are,

If we stay awake come what may ,

We will never be below par,

As these attributes we will display.

Even then we may nod off again,

Requiring we investigate once more,

This awakened level to regain,

Recognition of Awareness is the open door.

Poem Fifteen

Instrument of Consciousness

This poem shows how investigation of experience can reveal living organisms to be instruments of The Absolute, by which This can 'know' Itself.

Instrument of Consciousness

Sitting quietly one can attention direct,

On sensations which in the body appear,

Which the many nerves detect,

Of these, Awareness becomes the seer.

Also sounds detected by the ears,

Thus by Awareness these are 'seen',

Thoughts, noises in the mind that hears,

Aware of which we know they've been.

Sights detected by the eyes,

Thus of them we become aware,

Aromas in the nose arise,

So Awareness knows they're there.

Flavours by the buds are tasted,

Then are reflected on the 'screen',

Of Awareness, where images are 'pasted',

When by the mind they are seen.

So body/mind is an instrument,

Through which Awareness can sense,

And contemplate the immanent,

Or universe, so immense.

By which It can enjoy and engage,

With Its own manifestation,

Or the inner depths it can gauge,

By self-inquiry and meditation.

Thus consciousness can 'itself know',

In both modes, at rest or in vibration,

As Awareness or the object-flow,

Through body/mind, thought and sensation.

Poem Sixteen

Purpose and Meaning

This poem deals with purpose and meaning, and attempts to show that it is only when identified as a separate individual, living in an alien world, that life seems meaningless unless it is given an extrinsic 'purpose'.

Purpose and Meaning

All is Consciousness, at rest or at play,

The former Awareness, the unmanifest,

And creation, cosmic energy that may,

Be 'seen' in motion, ere returning to rest.

When awake 'we' can truly play the game,

With no-self we joyfully participate.

When 'asleep' we cannot do the same,

Identified as an object that is separate.

When the world is met with a still mind,

With no reference to an individual seer,

Its wonder and beauty we can find,

Needing no extra purpose for us to cheer.

As an instrument of Consciousness can

Creation experience and enjoy,

Mind/body is more useful than

A discrete object, or a cosmic toy.

All conscious beings fulfill this function,

Through which Awareness can participate,

And spontaneously live with no compunction,

Allowing Consciousness to Itself relate.

Amazement, awe and gratitude,

Are outcomes of seeing the world this way,

As Awareness without personal attitude,

There is no separation from the play.

It is only when identified with body or mind,

As a unique, separate human being,

Extra purpose or meaning we need to find,

For existence 'as it is' we are not seeing.

Poem Seventeen

On This and That

'This' and 'That' are both epithets for Universal Consciousness, - Awareness when at rest and Cosmic Energy when in motion.

On This and That

Overcome fear ... by seeing what's Here!

Forget about church ... Just give up the search!

No need for a prayer mat ... Already you are That!

No Me, No you! There's nothing to do ...

Nobody, No mind! There's nothing to find ...

No effort, No sweat! There's nothing to get ...

Wow! There's only Now...

Cheer! There's only Here...

How? Just Here and Now!

Just This! That's Bliss ...

Just Cease! That's Peace ...

Just Being! That's Freeing ....

Accept what is ... Then feel the kiss!

Live with no 'story'... Then all reveals its glory!

Each moment is enough ... The end of all Stuff!

Poem Eighteen

Nothing Has Essential Meaning

This poem investigates whether anything has essential meaning. That is whether any 'thing' has meaning with regard to our essential identity, who or what we are. It also addresses the major human problem of 'reading meaning into things that have no meaning'

Nothing Has Essential Meaning

There are many things that we are told,

Have meaning as to who, or what, we are,

Our body whether young or old,

Possessions, maybe even our fancy car!

Our occupation and astrology,

'Chinese year' and nationality.

Our religion and numerology,

Ancestry and personality.

It's true they influence the body/mind,

With which if we misidentify,

Makes it more difficult to find,

Awareness our true identity,

For each adds another layer,

Of separation and partition,

Which must be peeled away ere,

We awaken, thus completing our 'mission'.

So we must be careful not to read,

Meaning into things which come and go,

Thoughts and sensations which are the seed,

When clung to as 'ourselves', the ego.

At the deepest, fundamental level,

No things have essential meaning,

If not seen this our lives bedevil,

Clouding existence with its gleaning.

In fact we should studiously avoid,

Any thought which objectifies the 'I',

Which is pure Awareness and thus devoid

Of characteristics … the subjective 'eye'.

Poem Nineteen

Free Will ... Myth or Reality?

This poem discusses the question of whether we have free will to determine our essence, the deepest level of our being.

Free Will ... Myth or Reality?

Free will ... does such a thing exist?

This is an age old philosophical debate.

Yes, says the existentialist,

No! Determinists and nondualists state.

The former posit we are the body/mind,

And that our innate personality,

Can be by our will refined,

For 'we are what we choose ourselves to be'. (Sartre)

However, deeper than this body/mind

And the level of thought and sensation,

The conscious subjective essence we can find,

Ever aware of this manifestation.

At this level there is no separate being,

And thus no personal free will.

However, this is not so until we are seeing

This deepest 'ground', peaceful and still.

Until this is so we need to choose,

To investigate and uncover this 'ground',

To accomplish this we need to use,

Our will and intent 'til it is found.

So when identified with thought,

And feeling separation,

Free will exists and so we ought,

To investigate with determination.

Once the discovery has been made,

And with Awareness we become identified,

No personal will can be displayed,

For no separate being can we now find.

Poem Twenty

The Practical Application of Awakening

This poem attempts to debunk the myth that awakening can be detrimental to one's ability to cope with day to day life in the world.

Awakening is Immensely Practical

Awakening is immensely practical,

Transformative rather than tactical.

Existential angst does it banish,

This fear and anxiety totally vanish.

In this life unfolds with no personal 'story'.

Then manifestation appears in all its glory.

When the world is met with a clear mind,

So vivid and alive do it we find.

Every sensation comes on so strong,

When not filtered through what's 'right and wrong'.

Thus seeing things as they truly 'are'

Our opinionated ego cannot mar.

When each moment is directly met,

The past and future go we let.

When the mind is still it does not distort,

So our experience does not fall short.

Sat-Chit-Ananda is another name,

For the source and essence of this cosmic game.

Sat – 'What is', Chit – Awareness of this,

Ananda – of this awareness the Bliss.

When awake we respond, rather than react,

To each situation depending on the fact.

Spontaneously does the mind our problems solve,

If unclouded by self it will not 'revolve'.

So I urge you all to awake,

Abandon self-image the great fake.

Investigate, discover what's really here,

Leading to a life with no angst and fear!

Poem Twenty-One

You Ask For Proof

This poem was written in answer to a question who continually asked for proof of Awareness and nonduality.

You Ask For Proof

You ask for proof,

What more proof could there be?

That which lives and breathes in me,

Also lives and breathes in thee.

The Lover and Beloved are ever within and without,

Of this amazing Mystery there can be no doubt.

She feels every sensation that our bodies feel,

As we eat She partakes of every meal.

That which we hear and see,

Is also heard and seen by the Beloved, Thee.

All that we taste and smell,

Is sensed, through us, by Thee as well.

Every thought with which our minds resound,

In Thy infinite Cosmic Mind is found.

For behind every conscious body/mind,

The Seer, Knower and Enjoyer can we find.

Moreover, not a thought nor sensation escapes,

Without appearing in Thy universal 'tapes'.

Within each of us our experiences are 'recorded',

By which device awareness of them is afforded.

In this there can be no separate 'saying',

Manifestation is the Lover and Beloved playing.

What appears to us as 'you' and 'me',

Are wondrous instruments of the Beloved, Thee.

Between the Unmanifest and manifestation,

There can be no separation.

For the Lover and Beloved are already one,

 Appearing as the 'many' just for fun!

Poem Twenty-Two

Peace and Goodwill

A Christmas poem.

Peace on Earth Goodwill to Men

'Peace on Earth',

And 'Goodwill to Men',

Need a second birth,

As we awaken.

For each of us to be at peace,

We need to wake up from this trance,

Our ID as body/mind must cease,

As Spirit we can truly enjoy 'the dance'.

Spirit is always silent and still,

Thus it is ever peaceful and serene,

It activates these bodies that mill …

With no 'small self' life is so keen.

'Goodwill to Men' means universal love,

The outcome of seeing no separation,

In which none are 'below or above',

Awake this is so, with no manipulation.

So the birth of Christ let us celebrate,

An amazing awakened being,

Whose life did the truth demonstrate,

Devoted to his fellow humans 'freeing'.

A true man of peace and goodwill,

Who loved all as himself,

With joy and healing did he others fill,

Not leaving any 'on the shelf'.

So let us his wonderful example follow,

By awakening to the nondual reality.

Then our 'peace and goodwill' are not hollow,

For they will become our 'normality'.

www.ingramcontent.com/pod-product-compliance
Lightning Source LLC
Chambersburg PA
CBHW031422040426
42444CB00005B/677